APA Manual 7th Edition Simplified for Easy Citation

Concise APA Style Guide for Students

Student Citation Styles Series

Appearance Publishers
2021

APA Manual 7th Edition Simplified for Easy Citation
Concise APA Style Guide for Students

Student Citation Styles Series
Book 2

"APA Manual 7th Edition Simplified for Easy Citation" is accurately structured to clarify the basics and important aspects of the updated edition of the APA Publication Manual (APA 7th edition) and includes over 60 most important examples of different kinds of references to simplify the writing process for students.

Revised according to the 7th edition of the APA Manual, this guide is offering general format and examples of paper layout and main paper elements, such as title page, abstract, headings, in-text citations, quotations, reference list, tables and figures, appendices, etc. among others including APA student paper sample and APA professional paper sample. Learn more about writing style, language, and formatting.

This student guide reflects the newest version of the APA Publication Manual and will address the questions about using APA Style Guide 7th Edition correctly with 60+ examples of references.

© Copyright 2021 Appearance Publishers

All rights are reserved. No part of this publication may be reproduced in any form or stored in a retrieval system in any form or by any means without prior written permission from authors.

Includes bibliographical references.

Table of Contents

FOREWORD 6
1.0 APA INTRODUCTION 7
2.0 GENERAL GUIDELINES 8

   2.1 Paper Layout 8
   2.2 Page Header 8
   2.3 Fonts 9
   2.4 Major Paper Sections 9

      Title Page 9
      Abstract 14

   2.5 Headings 16

      Level 1 16
      Level 2 16
      Level 3 16
      Level 4 16
      Level 5 16

   2.6 Tables and Figures 17

      Tables 17
      Figures 20

3.0 IN-TEXT CITATIONS 22

   3.1 Basics 22

      Parenthetical and Narrative Citation 22
      Author-Date Method 23
      Titles of Sources within the Text 23

   3.2 Short Quotations 24
   3.3 Long Quotations (Blockquotes) 24
   3.4 Quotations from Sources without Pages 25
   3.5 Summary or Paraphrase 26
   3.6 Making Changes to Direct Quotes 26

      Shortening Quotes 26
      Clarifying Quotes 26

   3.7 General Format 27
   3.8 Examples 27

      1 Author 27
      2 Authors 27
      3+ Authors 27
      Organization as an Author 28
      Unknown Author 29
      Unknown Date 29
      2+ Works in the Same Parentheses 30
      Authors with the Same Last Names 30
      2+ Works by the Same Author in the Same Year 30
      Personal Communication 31
      Indirect Sources 31
      Sources without Page Numbers 31

   3.9 Quick Summary 32

4.0 REFERENCE LIST 33

   4.1 Formatting a Reference List 33

  Authors 33
  Titles 34
  DOI or URL 34
  Abbreviations in References 34
 4.2 Author / Authors 35
  1 Author 35
  2 Authors 35
  3 to 20 Authors 35
  20+ Authors 36
  2+ Works by the Same Author 36
  2+ Works by the Same Author / Same Year 38
  Group Author / Organization 39
  Unknown Author 39
 4.3 Books 40
  General Format 40
  Edition Other than the First 41
  Edited Book 41
  Chapter in an Edited Book 41
  Multivolume Book 42
  Electronic Book 42
 4.4 Articles in Periodicals 43
  General Format 43
  Article in Print Periodical 44
  Article in Electronic Periodical 44
  Article in Magazine 44
  Article in Newspaper 45
  Online Scholarly Journal Article 45
  Review 46
 4.5 Print Sources 47
  Dictionary / Encyclopedia (Group Author) 47
  Dictionary / Encyclopedia (Individual Author / Authors) 47
  Dissertation / Thesis 47
  Report 48
  Government Report 48
  Bible 48
 4.6 Online Sources 49
  Webpage 49
  Wikipedia 50
  Dictionary / Encyclopedia 51
  Dissertation / Thesis 51
  Graphic Data 52
  Online Presentation 52
  E-Mail 53
  Blog Post 53
  Facebook Post 53
  Instagram Post 54
  Tweet 54
 4.7 Audiovisual Sources 55
  YouTube 55
  TED Talk 55
  Film 56
  TV Series 56
  Song / Track 56
  Podcast 57

      Image 57
      Photograph 57
  4.8 Other Sources 58
      Published Interview 58
      Speech 59
      Conference 59
      Conference Proceedings 59
      Personal Communication 60

5.0 QUICK IN-TEXT / REFERENCE LIST EXAMPLES 61

  Book 61
  E-Book 61
  Chapter in an Edited Book 61
  Article in Periodical 62
  Webpage 62
  Dictionary 63
  Film 63
  TV Series 64
  YouTube 64
  TED Talk 65
  Image 65
  Tweet 66
  Government Report 66
  Bible 66

6.0 APPENDICES 67

  6.1 Formatting Appendices 67
  6.2 Text Appendices 68
  6.3 Table and/or Figure Appendices 68

7.0 APA SAMPLE PAPER 69

  7.1 Student Paper 70
  7.2 Professional Paper 79

SOURCES 88

FOREWORD

APA (The American Psychological Association)

This student guide reflects the newest version of the *American Psychological Association (APA) Publication Manual* (7th edition), which was released in October 2019.

Revised according to the 7th edition of the APA manual, this guide is offering examples on:

- General format of APA papers,
- In-text citations,
- Reference list,
- Tables/figures,
- Appendices,

including:

- APA student paper and
- APA professional paper samples.

This student guide will assist you learn how to use the American Psychological Association (APA) Style for references and citations.

This guide will address the vast majority of questions about using APA style correctly. However, if you are working on a complex document or if you require more information on specific area of APA Style, please consult the *Publication Manual of the American Psychological Association* (7th edition) or the APA Style website (https://apastyle.apa.org) for more details.

If you are a student, consult with your professor to find out what style your discipline requires prior to choosing APA Style for formatting your work.

Keep in mind: your instructor is the final authority on how to format your paper correctly.

Appearance Publishers
2021

1.0 APA INTRODUCTION

Referencing is acknowledging the copyrights of resources used in your academic writing, which gives all necessary information to identify the work cited within the text.

Any source that you have used and referred to in your academic writing must be:
1. Acknowledged in text (as in-text citation),
2. Included in reference list (as full reference).

As a rule, APA is most often used for the following disciplines:

- Social Sciences:
    - Psychology,
    - Sociology,
    - Linguistics,
    - Criminology,
- Business,
- Nursing.

2.0 GENERAL GUIDELINES

2.1 Paper Layout

APA manual has the following requirements for the paper layout:
- Standard paper, A4 format:
  - 8.5 inches x 11 inches,
- 1-inch margins on all sides,
- Page header at the top of every page:
  - For a professional paper, this includes your paper title and the page number.
  - For a student paper, this only includes the page number.
- Double-spaced text,
- The first line of every paragraph should be indented 0.5 inches.

2.2 Page Header

For student paper, to create a page header:	**For professional paper,** to create a page header:

1. Insert the page number, flush right.	1. Insert shortened title of the paper flush left, all capital letters:
	   - The title should be up to 50 characters in length and take only 1 line of text,
	   - Abbreviate long titles if needed.
	2. Insert the page number, flush right.

Example (for student paper):

	1

Example (for professional paper):

TITLE OF YOUR PAPER	1

2.3 Fonts

APA manual recommends to use standard available fonts:
- Serif fonts:
    - Times New Roman - 12pt.,
    - Georgia - 11pt., etc.
- Sans serif fonts:
    - Arial - 11pt.,
    - Calibri - 11pt., etc.

2.4 Major Paper Sections

Any APA-formatted research paper should include 4 major sections:
1. Title page,
2. Abstract,
3. Main body,
4. References.

Title Page

APA manual provides different requirements for formatting the title page / cover page for:
1. Student papers:
    - Intended for credit in a course,
2. Professional papers:
    - Intended for scholarly publication.

Student paper title page includes:	**Professional paper title page** includes:
1. A page header, 2. The title of the paper, 3. The name of each author of the paper, 4. The institutional affiliation for each author, 5. The course name and number, 6. The instructor's name and title, 7. The assignment's due date.	1. A page header, 2. The title of the paper, 3. The name of each author of the paper, 4. The affiliation for each author, 5. The author note (if applicable).

Elements of Title Page

	Student Paper Title Page Elements	Professional Paper Title Page Elements
General	All text should be double-spaced	
Header	Page number flush right at the top of the page	Running head with the page number flush right at the top of the page
Title	Title should be placed in the upper half of the page: • Title case, bold, centered • Title can take up to 2 lines	

Author(s)	The author's name includes first name, middle initials, and last name:
	• Do not use titles or degrees
	• List all the authors in order of contribution
	• For 2 authors, separate the names with "and":
	   o Laura L. Hernandez and Dennis Wilson
	• For 2+ authors, separate the names with commas and "and" for the last author's name:
	   o Laura L. Hernandez, Dennis Wilson, John Lee and Mia K. Anderson	

Author's Affiliation	Indicate the institution or location where the author conducted the research	
Course	Use the format used by the institution: Example: LIT 2012 Example: GOV 101	-
Instructor	Use the instructor's preferred form: Example: Dr. Anderson Example: Ms. Thomas	-
Assignment Due Date	Use the most common format: Example: March 4, 2021 Example: 4 March 2021	-

Author Note	-	An author note should appear in the bottom half of the page:
		- "Author note" is bold and centered
		- The paragraphs are left-aligned
		- The first line of each paragraph is indented 0.5 inches
		
		Author note is divided into 4 paragraphs:
		
		The 1st paragraph includes:
		   o The author's name
		   o The ORCID iD symbol
		   o The URL for the ORCID iD
		
		The 2nd paragraph indicates:
		   o Any change in affiliation
		   o Any deaths of the authors
		
		The 3rd paragraph includes:
		   o Disclosure of conflicts of interest
		   o Acknowledgement of financial and other support
		   o Study registration
		
		The 4th paragraph includes:
		   o Contact information

Example:

1

Modern Period in the English Literature:

Key Points about Modern Period

Marcus White

Department of English Literature, Heldens University

ELD 1201: Modern English Literature

Dr. Korsh

April 25, 2021

Professional Paper

Example:

MODERN PERIOD IN THE ENGLISH LITERATURE

Modern Period in the English Literature:

Key Points about Modern Period

Marcus White and White Andrew

English Literature Online Lab

Department of English Literature, Heldens University

Author Note

Marcus White https://orcid.org/1257-8436-2456

White Andrew https://orcid.org/4678-8926-3324

White Andrew is now at the Department of English History, Heldens University.

We have no conflicts of interests to disclose.

Correspondence concerning this article should be addressed to White Andrew, 34 E New Heldens St., North Hollick KB 302928. Email: whiteandrew@heldens.edu.

Abstract

The abstract is a 150-250-word concise summary of the key points of your paper:
- Begin the abstract on a separate page after the title page.
- Center and bold the label "Abstract".
- Your abstract should:
  - Be double-spaced,
  - Be single not indented paragraph,
  - Contain no more than 250 words.

Content

- Abstract should contain at least:
  - Research topic and questions,
  - Methods and results,
  - Data analysis,
  - Findings,
  - Conclusions.
- Additionally, you may:
  - Include possible implications of your research.
  - List paper's keywords:
    - Indent the first line 0.5 inches after the abstract paragraph.
    - Italicize "Keywords:".
    - Add 3-5 keywords in lowercase letters, not italicized, separated with commas.
    - Do not use a period after the final keyword.

Example:

Abstract

Lorem ipsum dolor sit amet, consectetur adipiscing elit. Vivamus id dapibus libero. Phasellus vel urna nisi. Orci varius natoque penatibus et magnis dis parturient montes, nascetur ridiculus mus. Curabitur ac luctus nisi, sed maximus nibh. Curabitur congue accumsan nisi, a sollicitudin turpis aliquam at. Phasellus suscipit est eget augue sagittis, ac lobortis ex egestas. Mauris vitae purus lacus. Proin imperdiet feugiat posuere. Sed a lacus aliquam, cursus sem et, faucibus nibh. Nulla diam diam, aliquam ac ante ac, blandit ultricies lectus. Sed vitae enim nisl. Praesent eu erat eget enim viverra sagittis. Nunc vel lacinia dolor, in fermentum neque. Donec consequat rutrum quam. Duis eget lacus mollis, gravida risus eu, auctor lorem. Donec sit amet libero nisi. Pellentesque sit amet ante rutrum, feugiat ipsum vel, ornare leo. Proin tincidunt purus ut massa aliquam, fermentum malesuada elit interdum. Sed posuere ut mauris non molestie. Integer nec condimentum mi, nec ornare nisi. Nulla non sagittis nibh. Suspendisse in felis at ipsum tristique pharetra sed in neque. Cras orci purus, pulvinar non placerat id, dapibus sed felis.

Keywords: Ipsum, purus, pulvinar

2.5 Headings

Headings are used to guide the reader through the text:
- The title of the paper is considered to be level 1 heading.
- Use the same font and spacing for all headings as for the text.
- Do not use letters or numbers for headings.
- Do not add extra lines above or below headings.
- Do not label introduction section with a heading:
  - For subsection in the introduction section, use level 2 heading.

Special headings are used for certain sections of a paper and are always positioned at the top of the new page, bold and centered:
- Abstract,
- Contents
- Title of Paper,
- References,
- Footnotes,
- Appendix.

There are 5 heading levels in APA:

Level 1

Centered, Bold, Title Case Heading
Text starts with a new paragraph.

Level 2

Flush left, Bold, Title Case Heading
Text starts with a new paragraph.

Level 3

Flush Left, Bold, Italic, Title Case Heading
Text starts with a new paragraph.

Level 4

Indented, Bold, Title Case Heading With a Period. Text continues on the same line/paragraph as the heading.

Level 5

Indented, Bold, Italic, Title Case Heading With a Period. Text continues on the same line/paragraph as the heading.

2.6 Tables and Figures

Tables and figures are optional visuals for the paper to structure the information and ease readers' understanding:
- Tables are any graphics that use rows and columns to structure the content.
- Figures are any visuals other than tables.

General Guidelines

- Number all tables sequentially.
- Number all figures sequentially.
- Each table and figure should be comprehensible without having to refer to the text:
    - Include explanation of every abbreviation.
- When citing the table or figure from another source, maintain the original structure.

Tables

Elements of tables:
- Numbers:
    - All tables should be numbered with Arabic numerals sequentially with the same order as they appear in the text:
        - Table 1,
        - Table 2, etc.
    - Numbers are bolded and left aligned.
- Titles:
    - The title of the table should be written in italicized title case below the number og the table.
    - Leave a blank line between the number and the title of the table.
- Headings:
    - All columns must have headings.
    - All headings should be written in sentence case.
- Body:
    - Short entries should be centered sentence case.
    - Longer entries should be left-aligned sentence case.
    - Leave cell blank if data were not obtained:
        - Put a dash in cell and a general note if needed to explain why the cell is blank.
- Spacing:
    - Use double spacing for:
        - The number of the table,
        - The title of the table,
        - Notes.
    - Use single, one and a half, or double spacing for:
        - The body of the table.
- Borders:

- Spacing and alignment is usually enough to clarify the cells:
    - Avoid using many horizontal lines,
    - Do not use any vertical lines,
- Include only horizontal lines that are needed for clarity to separate:
    - Column spanners,
    - Elements of a decked head,
    - Totals, etc.
- Do not use:
    - Vertical lines,
    - Borders around each cell.
- Notes:
    - Notes should supplement the content of the table and can be of the following types:
        1. General,
        2. Specific,
        3. Probability notes.
    - Notes should appear in the above-mentioned order below the table:
        - General notes provide citations or any additional information for the table in regards to units of measurement, symbols, abbreviations, etc.
        - Specific notes explain certain column, row, or element.
        - Probability notes clarify statistical significance of specific values.

Example:

Lorem ipsum dolor sit amet, consectetur adipiscing elit. Nam aliquam odio et arcu cursus lobortis. Curabitur commodo ipsum ac ullamcorper hendrerit. Phasellus volutpat urna in gravida dictum. Phasellus vitae nulla ligula.

Table 2

Title of Table Title Case

Stub Heading	Column Spanner 1		Column Spanner 2	
	Column Heading 1	Column Heading 2	Column Heading 3	Column Heading 4
Table Spanner 1				
Row 1	XXX	XXX[a]	XXX	XXX
Row 2	XXX	XXX	XXX	XXX
Table Spanner 2				
Row 3	XXX	XXX	XXX***	XXX
Row 4	XXX	XXX	XXX***	XXX

Note. A general note.

[a] A specific note.

*** A probability note.

Proin cursus massa urna, porttitor placerat turpis hendrerit vel. Mauris non sem viverra, suscipit purus vel, vulputate velit. Sed tellus quam, ultricies a cursus a, euismod non leo. Class aptent taciti sociosqu ad litora torquent per conubia nostra, per inceptos himenaeos.

Figures

Figures include all graphical information other than tables:
- Graphs and charts,
- Images and photos,
- Maps, etc.

Elements of figures:
- Numbers:
    - All figures should be numbered with Arabic numerals sequentially with the same order as they appear in the text:
        - Figure 1,
        - Figure 2, etc.
    - Numbers are bolded and left aligned.
- Title:
    - The title of the figure should be written in italicized title case below the number of the figure.
- Spacing:
    - The number and title of figure should be double spaced.
- Image (figure itself):
    - The image of the figure is positioned under the title.
    - The image of the figure should be of legible size and resolution.
    - Maintain consistent size of fonts:
        - Between 8 and 14 pt.
    - For headings and axis, use title case capitalization.
    - For descriptions, use sentence case capitalization.
- Legends:
    - The legends should be written in title case.
    - The legends should go within or under the image.
- Notes:
    - Notes should supplement the content of the figure and can be of the following types:
        1. General,
        2. Specific,
        3. Probability notes.
    - Notes should appear in the above-mentioned order below the figure:
        - General notes provide citations or any additional information for the figure in regards to units of measurement, symbols, abbreviations, etc.
        - Specific notes explain certain elements.
        - Probability notes clarify statistical significance of specific values.

Example:

Pellentesque imperdiet diam ligula, aliquam laoreet ante faucibus ut.. Aenean varius eros a nibh sagittis, id mattis diam rhoncus. Vestibulum maximus tincidunt metus ac congue.

Figure 2

Title of Figure Title Case

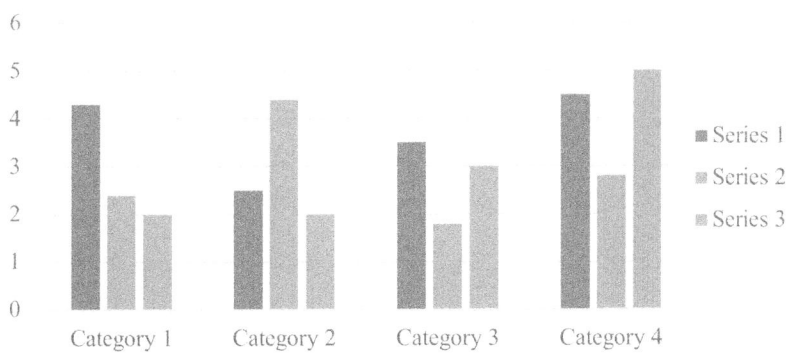

Note. General note explaining units of measurement, abbreviations, etc. or provide citation information.

Aenean ac felis eget magna dignissim sodales. Suspendisse imperdiet nisl et nisi condimentum pharetra. Proin vitae tellus semper, venenatis quam in, lobortis libero. Quisque tristique mauris fringilla ornare vehicula. Duis a odio erat.

3.0 IN-TEXT CITATIONS

The APA manual suggests that writers should use:
- The past simple tense or
- The present perfect tense.

Example:

Brown (2019) found…
Brown (2019) has found…

Alternatively, in case writing does not required traditional forms writer are still allowed to use:
- The present simple tense.

Example:

Brown (2019) finds…

3.1 Basics

Parenthetical and Narrative Citation

The in-text citation can be of 2 forms:
1. Parenthetical and
2. Narrative.

Parenthetical Citation

Example:

According to recent research… (Taylor, 2018).

Narrative Citation

Example:
Taylor (2018) notes that…

Author-Date Method

The author-date method should be followed for all in-text citation when using APA:
- The author's last name and the year of publication should always appear in the text:
    - (Martin, 2013).
- Page number of the used source may be omitted in the text in case you refer to a general idea from another work rather than directly quoting the material.
- Page number must be included to the citation when directly quoting the material:
    - Use the abbreviation "p." (for one page) or "pp." (for several pages) before including the page number(s).
    - Use a dash for page range:
        - (Perez, 2017, p. 199),
        - (Perez, 2017, pp. 199–201).
- Each source mentioned in the text must be listed in the reference list and vice versa.

Titles of Sources within the Text

- If you refer to the title of a source in the text, capitalize all words that are 4+ letters long:
    - *Wonder and Hope.*
- Capitalize short words that are nouns, verbs, pronouns, adjectives, and adverbs:
    - *Lighting New Horizon,*
    - *There is Hope to Love.*
- Capitalize both words in a hyphenated compound word:
    - *Broad-Minded Person.*
- Capitalize the first word after a dash or colon:
    - "Gendered Labor Migration: The Case of Indramayu Regency."
- If the title of the source is italicized in your reference list, italicize it and use title case capitalization when referring to the source in the text:
    - *The Real Home,*
    - *The Crown,*
    - *Moxie.*
- If the title of the source is not italicized in your reference list, use double quotation marks and title case capitalization when referring to the source in the text:
    - "The Balmoral Test."

3.2 Short Quotations

When directly quoting from a source, include:
1. The author,
2. Year of publication, and
3. Page number.

- Start the quotation with a signal phrase that includes the author's last name and the date of publication in parentheses (in brackets). Page number should be placed after the quotation (in brackets):

Example:

According to Harris (2018), "the anticipated benefits relate to the purchaser's judgment concerning product quality and ability of the commodity or service to perform certain tasks" (p. 29).

- Alternatively, the author's last name, the year of publication, and the page number can be placed in parentheses after the quotation (in brackets).

Example:

He stated, "The anticipated benefits relate to the purchaser's judgment concerning product quality and ability of the commodity or service to perform certain tasks" (Harris, 2018, p. 29), but she did not offer an explanation as to why.

3.3 Long Quotations (Blockquotes)

Direct quotations that are 40+ words long should be placed in a free-standing block. Quotation marks are omitted:
- Do not add extra blank line before/after the quotation.
- Start the quotation on a new line, indented 0.5 inch from the left margin.
- The entire quotation should be typed on the new margin and indented 0.5 inch.
- Double-space the entire quotation.
- The parenthetical citation should be placed after the punctuation mark.

> *Example:*
>
> Pellentesque imperdiet diam ligula, aliquam laoreet ante faucibus ut. Duis diam lectus, malesuada non sollicitudin id, pellentesque at diam. Phasellus convallis urna eget augue ullamcorper fringilla. Sanchez's (2019) study found the following:
>
>> In September 2017, a Brexit debate was held at the Society's Annual General Meeting to discuss the process of Brexit and how it might affect the lives of microbiologists. The Society's General Secretary, Professor Maggie Smith, was joined by Professor Graeme Reid, Chair of the Campaign for Science & Engineering, who is a member of the Government's High Level Forum on Science and Brexit; and Professor Nick Talbot, a mycologist from the University of Exeter, who sits on the Russell Group's Europe Advisory Group, which is in direct contact with the Brexit negotiators both from the UK side and the EU side. (p. 340)

3.4 Quotations from Sources without Pages

For the sources which do not have pages, you may reference another logical element (or a combination of elements) for the direct quotation to help readers find the cited part, such as:

- A paragraph,
- A chapter,
- A table, etc.

> *Example:*
>
> Lewis (2010) defined globalization as the spread of free-market capitalism to all parts of the world (paras. 6–7).
>
> … (Carroll, 2017, Table 2)
> … (Bains, 2002, 03:26)

3.5 Summary or Paraphrase

- Page numbers may be omitted when referring to a general idea of another work or paraphrasing another author's material. Include only the author and year of publication in your in-text reference:

Example:

According to Okoye (2018), globalization can be explained as an intensification of social relations worldwide through the linkage of distant localities.

3.6 Making Changes to Direct Quotes

Generally, a direct quotation should not be altered. However, in order to integrate the quote into the work, sometimes the changes are needed:
- As long as the meaning of the quote remains the same, the writer may:
    - Shorten quotes,
    - Clarify quotes.

Shortening Quotes

- Use an ellipsis (. . .) with a space before and after omitted words, phrases, or sentences to indicate that some part of the quote has been left out:

Example:

According to Thierfelder (2017), "other than making sure the economic interactions in the region are active and peaceful . . . the Silk Road will also act as an economic and infrastructure incentive" (p. 73).

Clarifying Quotes

- Use square brackets ([]) for adding a word, phrase, or sentence to clarify any unclear part of the quote:

Example:

In the view of Brakman (2008), "the [Senate election] results are in sync with states' presidential votes" (p. 56).

3.7 General Format

When referring to another author's work in the text use the following general format for an in-text citation.

General Format:

(Author, Year, p. #).
(Author, Year, pp. #–#).

3.8 Examples

1 Author

Example:

Research by Devarajan (2019) supports...

(Devarajan, 2019)

---

2 Authors

- If the work has 2 authors, name both authors each time you refer to the source:
    - Use the word "and" between the authors' names mentioned in the text.
    - Use the ampersand (&) in parentheses.

Example:

Research by Lakatos and Robinson (2019) shows...

(Lakatos & Robinson, 2019)

3+ Authors

- If the work has 3+ authors, name only the first author followed by "et al." each time you refer to the source:

Example:

(Lin et al., 2012)

Lin et al. (2012) offered...

- If there are several works with the same first authors' names:
    - To avoid ambiguity, list as many first authors' names as needed followed by "et al." to clearly identify the reference by its corresponding in-text citation:

Example:

If you reference 2 works of such authors:	*To avoid ambiguity, use the following examples for in-text citations:*
Nain, Okoye, Berthou, Jardet, and Szczerbowicz (2020)	(Nain, Okoye, Berthou, et al., 2020)
Nain, Okoye, Siena, Brakman, and Thierfelder (2020)	(Nain, Okoye, Siena, et al., 2020)

- As long as "et al." is plural, it should always replace 2+ authors' names:
    - If there is only one author's name left to replace with "et al.", write the author's name instead.

Organization as an Author

- If the author is an organization, replace the author's name with the organization name for an in-text citation and treat the organization as the author:

Example:

According to the American Psychological Association (2019),...

- If the organization has an abbreviation, add the abbreviation in square brackets after the full organization name the first time the source is referred and then use only the abbreviation in following citations:

Example:	
First citation:	(American Civil Liberties Union [ACLU], 2014)
Second citation:	(ACLU, 2014)

Unknown Author

- When the source does not have an author, refer to the work by its full or shortened title instead of author's name:
    - Titles of books and reports should be italicized.
    - Titles of articles, chapters, and web pages should be put in quotation marks.

Example:
Other than making sure the economic interactions in the region are active and peaceful the Silk Road will also act as an economic and infrastructure incentive ("Making Changes," 2016).

- APA manual suggests to treat "Anonymous" as the author's name and use the name "Anonymous" as the author in the reference list as well:
    - (Anonymous, 2001).

Unknown Date

- If no date of publication is known, use the abbreviation "n.d." (no date) instead of date:

Example:
The nurses also plan referrals, discharge process and do follow-ups to facilitate the success of the treatment processes ("Heart Care," n.d.).

2+ Works in the Same Parentheses

- If you refer to 2+ works by different authors within a single citation, order them alphabetically and separate by a semi-colon.

Example:

(Boom, 2020; Code, 1999)

- If you refer to 2+ works by the same author within a single citation, give the author's name once and follow with dates:
    - Dates order: "No date" go first, then years, then "in-press".

Example:

(Yeung, n.d., 1999, 2018, in press)

Authors with the Same Last Names

- Use the author's initials along with the last name for in-text citation to prevent confusion. Separate citations by a semi-colon:

Example:

(E. Johnson, 2001; L. Johnson, 1998)

2+ Works by the Same Author in the Same Year

- If you have to cite 2+ sources by the same author in the same year, use lower-case letters (a, b, c, …) after the year to order the entries and prevent confusion:

Example:

Research by Guo (2013a) revealed weak possibility. However, another study (Guo, 2013b) resulted in…

Personal Communication

- For person-to-person communication (interviews, letters, e-mails, etc.), cite the communicator's name, state that it is a personal communication, and include the full date of the conducted communication:
  - According to APA manual, personal communication should not be added in the reference list.

Example:

(S. Schultz, personal communication, January 12, 2021).

Indirect Sources

- If you cite a source that was initially cited in another source, name the original source in a signal phrase:
  - Include the secondary source in the in-text citation with the words "as cited in".
  - Include the year of the original source in the in-text citation.

Example:

Cosman offered... (as cited in McAlister, 2016, p. 34).

(Cosman, 2001, as cited in McAlister, 2016, p. 34).

Sources without Page Numbers

- When a source does not have pages, include any other relevant element (or a combination of elements) that will help readers find the cited part:
  - A paragraph,
  - A chapter,
  - A table, etc.:

Example:

(Bacon, 1999, Chapter 6)
(Cardiac Rehabilitation Registry section, 2008, para. 2)
(Arthur, 2009, Slide 36)

3.9 Quick Summary

Author Type	Parenthetical Citation	Narrative Citation
1 author	(Parsons, 2021)	Parsons (2021)
2 authors	(Parsons & Grace, 2021)	Parsons and Grace (2021)
3+ authors	(Parsons et al., 2021)	Parsons et al. (2021)
Organization as an author	(Macmillan Dictionary, 2021)	Macmillan Dictionary (2021)
Abbreviated group author		
• First citation	(American Civil Liberties Union [ACLU], 2021)	American Civil Liberties Union (ACLU, 2021)
• Subsequent citations	(ACLU, 2021)	ACLU (2021)
Same author / same date	(Parsons, 2021a, 2021b)	Parsons (2021a, 2021b)
Same surname authors	(A. Parsons, 2021; B. Parsons, 2020)	Alan Parsons (2021) and Bella Parsons (2020)
Multiple works	(Heise, 2018; Port of Vancouver, 2017; Wee et al., 2021)	Wee et al. (2021), Heise (2018), and Ports of Vancouver (2017)

4.0 REFERENCE LIST

This chapter gives basic guidelines for formatting the reference list.

Reference List vs. Bibliography

A reference list includes only the sources you refer to in your writing.

A bibliography includes all the sources used during the research for background reading including those which were not mentioned in the text itself.

The purpose of creating the reference list is to let your readers find all the sources you used:
- All references cited in the text must appear in the reference list and vice versa.

Do not include references for:
- Sources that you only consulted for background reading,
- General mentions of websites or periodicals,
- Personal communications,
- Common knowledge.

4.1 Formatting a Reference List

Reference list should appear on a separate page at the end of your paper:
- Label "References" in bold, centered, and at the top of the page.
- All references should be double-spaced.
- All lines after the first line of each entry should be indented 0.5 inch from the left margin (hanging indentation).
- Each source cited in the text must appear in reference list and vice versa.

References are ordered alphabetically by authors' last names:
- If the author is unknown, order the reference entry by the first word of the title ignoring articles "the", "a", and "an".

Authors

- All authors' names should be inverted (last names should go first).
- Authors' first and middle names should be written as initials.
- List up to 20 authors of a particular source:
  - Each author's name and initials should be separated from the next author with a comma.
  - Use an ampersand (&) before the last author's name.
  - If there are 21 or more authors, use an ellipsis (…) after the 19th author, and then the final author's name (with no ampersand).
- For several sources by the same author, list the entries in chronological order by the date of publication.

Titles

- For the titles of books, chapters, articles, reports, webpages, capitalize only:
    - The first letter of the first word of the title and subtitle,
    - The first word after a colon or a dash, and
    - Proper nouns.
- The titles of longer works should be italicized:
    - Books,
    - Collections,
    - Newspapers.
- The titles of shorter works should NOT be italicized:
    - Chapters in books,
    - Essays.

DOI or URL

- Works that can be accessed online should have a DOI or URL:
    - A DOI (digital object identifier) is an identification number that never changes and links reader to the document on the Internet.
    - A DOI is preferred over a URL.
    - Include the protocol (http:// or https://) for the DOI and URL:
        - DOI must always be presented in the format https://doi.org/xxxx.xxxx.xxxx
    - Do not add a period (.) after the DOI or URL.

Abbreviations in References

- Common parts of sources are abbreviated to save space in reference entries:

Revised edition	–	Rev. ed.
Second edition	–	2nd ed.
Editor / Editors	–	Ed. / Eds.
Translator / Translators	–	Trans. / Trans.
Narrator / Narrators	–	Narr. / Narrs.
No date	–	n.d.
Page / Pages	–	p. / pp.
Paragraph	–	para.
Volume / Volumes	–	Vol. / Vols.
Number	–	No.
Supplement	–	Suppl.

4.2 Author / Authors

The following guidelines apply to all kinds of sources listed in the reference list.

1 Author

- Author's last name, followed by author's initials (if any).

Example:

Garcia, H. (2019). *The boy who harnessed the wind.* Hachette Livre.

2 Authors

- List authors' last names, followed by initials.
- Separate authors' names with a comma.
- Use an ampersand (&).

Example:

Roberts, E. R., & Mitchell, G. N. (2014). Binary stars as the key to understanding planetary nebulae. *Nature Communications, 34*(5), 34-36.

http://dx.doi.org/1024.3463.5540/x056k

3 to 20 Authors

- List authors' last names, followed by initials.
- Separate authors' names with a comma.
- The last author's name is preceded by ampersand.

Example:

Gray, E., Edwards, F. V., Stewart, A. T., Cook, G. H., & King, C. (2014). The

concurrent emergence and causes of double volcanic hotspot tracks on the

Pacific plate. *Nature Communications, 37*(2), 104-107.

http://dx.doi.org/1124.3463.3544/xk7rs

20+ Authors

- Any reference entry should have no more than 20 authors' names in total.
- List authors' last names, followed by initials.
- Separate authors' names with a comma.
- After the first 19 authors' names, use an ellipsis (. . .) in place of the remaining authors' names.
- The last author's name is NOT preceded by ampersand.

Example:

Green, A., Collins, F., Wright, D., Collins, H., Miller, B., Reed, G., Morgan, F. L.,

Green, V., Anderson, C., Adams, D., Li, Q., Scott, R., Hernandez, T. K.,

Walker, C., Baker, A. K., Evans, T. T. R., Morris, B. O., Brown, B., White,

M., . . . Murphy, E. K. (2010). Molecular mechanisms underlying the

evolution of the signalosome. *Science Advances, 54*(7), 22-26.

http://dx.doi.org/1544.3463.4540/drky77

2+ Works by the Same Author

- Order several sources with the same author by the year of publication:
    - "n.d." comes first,
    - then dates (earliest one comes first),
    - then "in press".

> *Example:*
>
> Parker, R. T. (n.d.)...
>
> Parker, R. T. (1999)...
>
> Parker, R. T. (2012a)....
>
> Parker, R. T. (2012b, May)...
>
> Parker, R. T. (in press)...

- If the same author is a sole author of one work and is the first author of another group-work, list the one-author entry first.

> *Example:*
>
> Campbell, N. H. (Ed.). (2015). *Methods for in vitro evaluating antimicrobial activity:*
>
> *A review*. Houghton Mifflin Harcourt.
>
> Campbell, N. H., & Edwards, E. Y. (Eds.). (2015). *Tunnelling spectroscopy of*
>
> *Andreev states in graphene*. Pearson Education.

- For the references that have the same first author and different following authors, order the entries alphabetically.

> *Example:*
>
> Phillips, V. C., Campbell, S., Johnson, F. T., Hall, T. Y., & Lopez, H. (2017). The
>
> Rohingya people of Myanmar: Health, human rights, and identity.
>
> *International Journal of Clean Coal and Energy, 56*(8), 23-31.

Phillips, V. C., Rogers, F. L., Green, T. D., Baker, V., & Harris, D. D. (2017).

Charting organellar importomes by quantitative mass spectrometry.

International Journal of Geosciences, 1(2), 34-56.

2+ Works by the Same Author / Same Year

- For the references by the same author and published in the same year, check if there are more specific publication dates:
    - Works with only a year are listed before specific dates.
    - Order references with specific dates chronologically.
- If several references have the same publication date:
    - Order them alphabetically by the title coming after the date of publication.
    - Assign letters (a, b, c, …) to the year to avoid confusion when referring to the sources in the text.

Example:

Wright, F. R. (2015a). Branched-chain and aromatic amino acids in relation to behavioral problems among young Inuit from Nunavik, Canada: A cohort study. *International Journal of Organic Chemistry, 7*(6), 8-12.

Wright, F. R. (2015b). Chemokine profiles of interstitial pneumonia in patients with dermatomyositis: A case control study. *International Journal of Medical Physics, Clinical Engineering and Radiation Oncology, 12*(5), 6-7.

Group Author / Organization

- Group authors (referred to as "organization") can include:
    - Corporations,
    - Government agencies,
    - Organizations, etc.
- Treat the organization as the author's name and format the rest of reference as normal.
- Give the full name of the group author in your reference list:
    - Abbreviations may be used only in the text.

Example:

Canadian Oxford Dictionary. (2012). Heritage. In *Canadian Oxford Dictionary*.

    Houghton Mifflin Harcourt.

Unknown Author

- If the source does not have an author, move the title of work to the place of author's name.
- Use "Anonymous" if the author of the work is signed as "Anonymous.".

Example:

New Oxford Dictionary of English (7th ed.). (2019). Oxford University Press.

- Use a shortened title of work when referring to the source without author in the text:
    - For example, in-text citation of the source given in example above would be: (New Oxford Dictionary, 2019).

4.3 Books

- APA manual requires DOIs for all books that have one (whether printed or digital).

General Format

General Format:
Author, A. A. (Year). *Title of book: Subtitle of book* (Edition). Publisher. DOI

Author, A. A.:
   List each author's last name and initials as Author, A. A., Author, B. B., & Author, C. C. Use an ampersand (&) before the final author's name.
Year:
   Include year of publication.
***Title of work: Subtitle of work*:**
   Italicize the title and capitalize the first word of the title and subtitle and any proper nouns.
Edition:
   Include edition in parentheses if available.
Publisher:
   Do not include the publisher location.
DOI:
   Include DOI if available using the format https://doi.org/xxxx.xxxx.xxxx.

Example:
Coleman, J. (2001). *Small girl dreaming: The chocolate touch*. Bonnier Books.
Simmons, U. E., & Griffin, A. J. (2019). *Polymer nanotechnology: Nanocomposites* (3rd ed.). John Wiley & Sons.

Edition Other than the First

General Format:	Author, A. A. (Year). *Title of book: Subtitle of book* (Edition). Publisher. DOI
Example:	Powell, I. (2020). *Precision Radiology: Predicting longevity using feature engineering and deep learning methods in a radiomics framework* (4th ed.). Grupo Santillana.

Edited Book

General Format:	Author, A. A. (Year). *Title of book: Subtitle of book* (A. A. Editor, Ed.). Publisher. (Original work published Year) DOI
Example:	Bennett, B. (2014). *Methods for evaluating antimicrobial activity* (P. J. C. Hughes, Ed.). Kodansha. (Original work published 1997)

Chapter in an Edited Book

General Format:	Author, A. A. (Year). Title of chapter. In A. A. Editor (Ed.), *Title of book: Subtitle of book* (pp. #-#). Publisher. DOI

Example:	Simmons, X. (2017). Imaging modes of atomic force microscopy. In H. J. Washington & R. Y. Ross (Eds.), *Biology: Application in molecular and cell biology* (pp. 193-198). Cengage Learning.

Multivolume Book

General Format:	Author, A. A. (Year). *Title of book: Subtitle of book* (Edition, Vol. #). Publisher. DOI
Example:	James, S., & Henderson, L. (2021). *Remote carboxylation: Halogenated aliphatic hydrocarbons with carbon dioxide* (12th ed., Vol. H). Macmillan Publishers.

Electronic Book

- If the physical book is published as an eBook or audiobook, it is only necessary to distinguish between the eBook or audiobook and the print version if the content is different:

General Format:
Author, A. A. (Year). *Title of book*. Publisher. URL
Author, A. A. (Year). *Title of book* [eBook edition]. Publisher. URL
Author, A. A. (Year). *Title of book* (A. A. Narrator, Narr.) [Audiobook]. Publisher. URL

4.4 Articles in Periodicals

- For the titles of articles capitalize only:
  - The first letter of the first word of the title and subtitle,
  - The first word after a colon or a dash, and
  - Proper nouns.
- The periodical title is title case and italicized.
- The volume number is also italicized.
- If a DOI (or URL) has been assigned to the article, include it after the page range:
  - Include a DOI even when using the print article.

General Format

General Format:

Author, A. A. (Year). Title of article. *Title of Periodical, Volume*(Issue), pages. DOI

Author, A. A.:
  List each author's last name and initial as Author, A. A., Author, B. B., & Author, C. C. Use an ampersand (&) before the final author's name.

Year:
  Include year of publication.

Title of article:
  Capitalize only first word and proper nouns for the title of article.

***Title of Periodical*:**
  Italicize and capitalize each long word in the periodical.

***Volume*:**
  Italicize the periodical volume number.

Issue:
  If there is an issue number, include it in parentheses, not italicized.

pages:
  Include page(s) of the periodical.

DOI:
  Include DOI if available using the format https://doi.org/xxxx.xxxx.xxxx.

Example:

Scott, N. S., Reed, E., Evans, T. O., & Thomas, V. (2008). Why some believe that global warming is a hoax. *Green and Sustainable Chemistry, 53*(3), 28–33. https://doi.org/10.1034596/lgk049f-3377

Article in Print Periodical

General Format:	Author, A. A. (Year). Title of article. *Title of Periodical, Volume*(Issue), pages.
Example:	Nelson, Y. (2019). Endangered species. *Graphene, 23*(5), 16–26.

Article in Electronic Periodical

General Format:	Author, A. A. (Year). Title of article. *Title of Periodical, Volume*(Issue), pages. DOI or URL
Example:	Rivera, W., & Mitchell, Q. (2016). The consequences of Brexit for European values. *International Journal of Communications, Network and System Sciences, 9*(6), 19–21. https://doi.org/10.5840/0404959566

Article in Magazine

General Format:	Author, A. A. (Year). Title of article. *Title of Magazine, Volume*(Issue), pages.
Example:	Roberts, C. (2015). How benefits can make your employees happy. *Brain Science, 12*(6), 307–321.

Article in Newspaper

General Format:	Author, A. A. (Year). Title of article. *Title of Newspaper, Volume*(Issue), pages.
Example:	Clark, L. (2021). Taxation aim to small businesses. *The Economy, 14*, 36–39.

Online Scholarly Journal Article

- Provide a DOI, when it is available:
    - If an online scholarly journal article has no DOI and is published online, include the URL instead with the date retrieved.

Online Scholarly Article (with DOI)

General Format:	Author, A. A. (Year). Title of article. *Title of Periodical, Volume*(Issue), pages. DOI
Example:	Williams, N., Morris, O., & Davis, S. F. (2020). How climate has changed. *Journal of Geographic Information System, 55*(13), 14A-14F. https://doi.org/55940.30495/x0495.065

Online Scholarly Article (no DOI)

General Format:	Author, A. A. (Year). Title of article: Subtitle of article. *Database.* Retrieved Month Day, Year, from URL

Example:	Reed, B. (2013). Preventing terrorist attacks. *ScienceOpen*. Retrieved March 21, 2021, from https://www.scienceopen.com/95049/title/005943

Review

General Format:	Author, A. A. (Year). Title of review. [Review of the book *Title of book: Subtitle of book*, by A. A. Author]. *Title of Periodical, Volume*(Issue), pages.
Example:	Cox, U. (2021). Adoption law [Review of the book *Various laws: Abortion around the world*, by Y. U. Gonzalez & C. C. Bailey]. *Building Construction and Planning Research, 41*(2), 35–39.

4.5 Print Sources

Dictionary / Encyclopedia (Group Author)

General Format:	Organization. (Year). Title of entry. In *Title of work* (Edition, pp. #-#). Publisher.
Example:	Longman. (2013). Homeschooling. In *Longman dictionary of contemporary English* (5h ed., pp. 304-305). Longman.

Dictionary / Encyclopedia (Individual Author / Authors)

General Format:	Author, A. A. (Year). Title of entry. In A. A. Editor (ed.), *Title of work* (Edition, pp. #-#). Publisher.
Example:	Bryant, X. G. (2020). Torrenting sites influence creativity and copyright. In H. U. Roberts (ed.), *Concise Oxford English dictionary* (pp. 406-409). Oxford University Press.

Dissertation / Thesis

General Format:	Author, A. A. (Year). *Title of dissertation/thesis* (Publication No. #) [Type of dissertation/thesis, University]. Database Name.
Example:	Thompson, K. V. (2014). *Effective ways of reducing air pollution* (Publication No. 2350968) [Doctoral dissertation, University of Toronto]. OpenDOAR.

- If the published dissertation or thesis is not published in a database, include the URL to locate the document.

Report

General Format:	Author, A. A. (Year). *Title of report.* Organization Name. URL
Example:	Richardson, M., Baker, H., Jackson, I., & Robinson, O. (2017). *Etsy SEO for vintage sellers 2016.* SEOarts. https://www.seoarts.com/vintage/report/title00349

Government Report

General Format:	Organization. (Year). *Title of report: Subtitle of report.* URL
Example:	United States Foundation for an Ecologically and Socially Just World. (2021). *Report: Self-awareness 2020.* https://www.usf-es.gov/reports/2020/file993039

Bible

General Format:	*Bible Version Title.* (Year). Publisher.
Example:	*The English Standard Version Bible.* (2001). Crossway.

4.6 Online Sources

- Electronic citations use square brackets to add specific information.
- Include month and date to the year of publication if possible.
- The label "Retrieved from" is no more in use for URLs or DOIs:
    - Retrieval date may still be used for the sources that are likely to change over the time.

Webpage

General Format:	Author, A. A. (Year, Month Day). *Title of webpage.* Website name. URL
Example:	Evans, U. (2020, May 16). *Eaton 72400-RGH-04 72400 series.* EATON. https://www.eaton.com/tw/en-us/skuPage.72400-RGH-04.html

- If the source is written by a group of authors (organization), use the name of the group/organization.

General Format:	Organization. (Year, Month Day). *Title of webpage.* Website name. URL
Example:	American Psychological Association. (2020, July 15). *Psychology topics.* APA. https://www.apa.org/topics

- If the author is unknown, use the title instead.
- Include a retrieval date if the source's content is likely to change over the time.

General Format:	*Title of webpage.* (Year, Month Day). Website name. Retrieved Month Date, Year, from URL
Example:	*APA format citation guide.* (2017, August 24). Mendeley. Retrieved March 24, 2021, from https://www.mendeley.com/guides/apa-citation-guide

- If the date of publication is not available, use the abbreviation "n.d." instead.

General Format:	Author, A. A. (n.d.). *Title of webpage.* Website name. URL
Example:	NASA. (n.d.). *Overview: Weather, global warming and climate change.* NASA. https://climate.nasa.gov/resources/global-warming-vs-climate-change/

Wikipedia

- Since the Wikipedia articles are likely to change over time, include the URL of archived page of the website:
    - Access the archived version by clicking "View History" and choosing the date/timestamp of the version you use for reference.

General Format:	Title of article. (Year, Month Day). In *Wikipedia.* URL of archived page
Example:	Geology. (2021, March 21). In *Wikipedia.* https://en.wikipedia.org/w/index.php?title=Geology&oldid=1014011568

Dictionary / Encyclopedia

- As long as online dictionary or encyclopedia are continuously updated, use "n.d." for the date of publication and include the retrieval date.

General Format:	Organization. (Year). Title of entry. In *Title of work*. URL
Example:	Macmillan Dictionary. (n.d.). Education. In *Macmillan Dictionary*. Retrieved March 27, 2021, from https://www.macmillan.com.au/dictionary/education

OR

General Format:	Author, A. A. (Year). Title of entry. In A. A. Editor (Ed.), *Title of work* (edition). Publisher. DOI or URL
Example:	Morris, C. (n.d.). Scholastic. In X. U. Schintler & I. I. McNeely (Eds), *Random house dictionary of the English language*. HarperCollins. https://doi.org/10.3526/gk-5930-00695

Dissertation / Thesis

General Format:	Author, A. A. (Year). *Title of dissertation/thesis* (Publication No. #) [Type of dissertation/thesis, University]. Database Name.

Example:	Lopez, V. J. (2015). *Political trust and distrust in Japan.* (Publication No. 2349543) [Doctoral dissertation, University of Vancouver]. Public Library of Science.

Graphic Data

General Format:	Organization. (Year) [Description of graphic data]. Retrieved Month Day, Year, from URL
Example:	Google. (2013). [Google Map of Vancouver port]. Retrieved February 24, 2021, from https://www.google.com/maps/@49.2890976,-123.1111088,17.05z

Online Presentation

- For online presentations, provide the file format in square brackets:
    - Word document,
    - PowerPoint slides, etc.

General Format:	Author, A. A. (Year, Month Day). *Title of presentation* [File format]. Publisher. URL
Example:	Roberts, D. (2020, January 16). *Environmental studies* [PowerPoint slides]. Chasings. https://www.chasings.com/presentations/rtitle/00948606

E-Mail

- E-mail is treated as personal communication. Therefore, e-mails are not included in the list of references, but are only cited in the text:

Example:
(E. Robbins, personal communication, February 15, 2021).

Blog Post

General Format:	Author, A. A. (Year, Month Day). Title of post. *Publisher*. URL
Example:	Jenkins, I. (2020, May 26). Remote carboxylation of halogenated aliphatic hydrocarbons with carbon dioxide. *DFG*. https://www.dfg.edu/listtitle/0039485

Facebook Post

- If the Facebook post includes visuals, indicate type of post in square brackets:
  - Image,
  - Video, etc.

General Format:	Author, A. A. (Year, Month Day). *Text of Facebook post* [Type of post]. Facebook. URL
Example:	Global Trade. (2014, March 30). *Discover a world of trade opportunities in one place with detailed information about imports, market dynamics, tariffs* [Image attached]. Facebook. https://www.facebook.com/GlobalTrade/photos/a.24520469873-0978-vffj=typeA

Instagram Post

General Format:	Author, A. A. [@username]. (Year, Month Day). *Text of Instagram post* [Type of post]. Instagram. URL
Example:	Bob Jean [@bobjean_9]. (2014, July 21). *Looking back* [Photograph]. Instagram. https://www.instagram.com/p/sdFhngWoAHlvjf/

Tweet

- If the tweet includes visuals, indicate type of tweet in square brackets:
    - Tweet,
    - Image,
    - Video, etc.

General Format:	Author, A. A. [@username]. (Year, Month Day). *Text of tweet* [Tweet]. Twitter. URL
Example:	Thompson, U. [@thompdoct_1]. (2018, August 12). *You have got to be kidding...* [Tweet]. Twitter. https://twitter.com/thompdoct_1/status/346082768072582580

4.7 Audiovisual Sources

"Audiovisual source" refers to any kind media that contains:
- Audio components,
- Visual components, or
- A combination of both.

YouTube

- If the author's name is different from the YouTube username, include that username in square brackets.

General Format:	Author, A. A. [Username]. (Year, Month Day). *Title of video* [Video]. YouTube. URL
Example:	Gonzales, F. [Korab Lushi]. (2020, April 19). *Two steps from hell* [Video]. YouTube. https://www.youtube.com/watch?v=_FkvjJgl-fkd

TED Talk

General Format:	Author, A. A. (Year, Month Day). *Title of talk* [Video]. TED. URL
Example:	Simmons, L. (2019, September 15). *Letting go of God* [Video]. TED. https://www.ted.com/talks/julia_sweeney_letting_go_of_god

Film

General Format:	Director, A. A. (Director). (Year). *Title of film* [Film]. Production Company.
Example:	Butler, O. (Director). (2015). *The departed* [Film]. Walnut Creek.

TV Series

General Format:	Executive Producer, A. A. (Executive Producer). (Year-Year). *Title of series* [TV series]. Production Company.
Example:	Richardson, B. (Executive Producer). (2018-present). *Life on Mars* [TV series]. Warner Bros. Pictures.

Song / Track

- Recording artist or composer is considered as the author.

General Format:	Artist, A. A. (Year). Title of song [Song]. On *Title of album* [Album]. Record label.
Example:	Turner, N. (2020). Skins [Song]. On *Leather gang* [Album]. Rip Media Group.

Podcast

General Format:	Executive Producer, A. A. (Executive Producer). (Year-Year). *Title of podcast* [Audio podcast]. Production Company. URL
Example:	Mitchell, J. (Executive Producer). (2019-present). *Danish political saga* [Audio podcast]. Virgin Records. https://www.newworld-podcast.com/999800

Image

General Format:	Author, A. A. (Year). *Title of image* [Image]. Website name. URL
Example:	Lewis, A. (2020). *Proof found* [Image]. Borgen. https://borgen.com.au/images/title/0049

Photograph

- If the photograph does not have a title, briefly describe it with your own words and use the description instead of title:
  - Put the description of photograph in square brackets.

General Format:	Photographer, A. A. (Year). Title of photograph [Photograph]. *Publisher*. URL Photographer, A. A. (Year). [Description of photograph] [Photograph]. *Publisher*. URL
Example:	Lee, U. (2021). [Striking men] [Photograph] *The Washington Post*. https://www.washingtonpost.com/article/440395

4.8 Other Sources

Published Interview

- For the interview published online, use the format of referencing its medium.

General Format:	Author, A. A. (Year, Month Day). Title of interview. *Title of Periodical, Volume*(Issue), pages. URL
Example:	Brown, P. (1999, June 13). David Lawrence: Domestic gender violence is on the rise. *Intelligent Information Management, 9*(3), 5-7. https://intellgems.com/journal/2134499

- For the audio interview published in a database, treat the interviewee as the author:

General Format:	Author, A. A. (Year, Month Day). *Title of interview* [Interview]. Database. URL
Example:	Scott, U. (2011, July 15). *Evans Robert rare interview* [Interview]. Education Resources Information Center. https://educresor.com/articles/44052056-465

Speech

General Format:	Author, A. A. (Year, Month Day). *Title of speech* [Speech audio recording]. Website Name. URL
Example:	Martin, V. (2020, Dec. 23). *Using animals to conduct research experiments is wrong* [Speech audio recording]. Profit. https://profit.com.au/speech-titanium/678328

Conference

General Format:	Author, A. A. (Year, Month Day). *Title of presentation* [Type of presentation]. Title of Conference, Location. URL
Example:	Young, X. (2014, Oct. 30). *How has the institution of marriage changed in the postmodern world?* [Conference session]. Marriage Institution 2014 Conference, New York, NY, United States. https://www.youtube.com/watch?v=hjkdfmrRH8G

Conference Proceedings

General Format:	Author, A. A. (Ed.). (Year). *Title of proceedings*. Publisher. URL
Example:	Howard, X., Carter, A., & Taylor, G. (Eds.). (2009). *Proceedings of the 5th annual business conference on a successful startup*. Springer Nature. https://springer-nature.com/titles/efhdfkgfjjfl=sdghj3446

Personal Communication

Personal communication is any kind of communication that cannot be retrieved by a reader:
- Emails,
- Phone conversations, etc.

Personal communications are not included in the reference list:
- Instead, cite personal communications in the text:
    - Include the communicator's name,
    - Add the label "personal communication",
    - Include the date of the communication.

Example:

(I. Torres, personal communication, February 12, 2020).

- For referencing personal communication in a footnote, use the same format:

Example:

[1] K. Peterson (personal communication, March 14, 2021) also claimed that many of her students had difficulties with APA style.

APA manual does not require to cite personal communications. However, **it is a good practice** to locate a source if possible.

5.0 QUICK IN-TEXT / REFERENCE LIST EXAMPLES

Book

General Format:	Author, A. A. (Year). *Title of book: Subtitle of book* (Edition). Publisher.
Reference List:	Jackson, H. (2012). *Strategies today: The best strategy to build a house.* Penguin Random House.
In-text Citation:	(Jackson, 2012, p. 34)

E-Book

General Format:	Author, A. A. (Year). *Title of book: Subtitle of book.* Publisher. DOI or URL
Reference List:	Martin, E. (2013). *The house of mirth: Going up.* Hachette Livre. https://amzn.to/V48hdKso
In-text Citation:	(Martin, 2013, paras. 5-8)

Chapter in an Edited Book

General Format:	Author, A. A. (Year). Title of chapter. In A. A. Editor (Ed.), *Title of book: Subtitle of book* (pp. #-#). Publisher. DOI
Reference List:	Thompson, A. (2019). Practical knowledge. In V. Hall & P. Allen (Eds.), *Chasing the time* (pp. 40–52). Simon & Schuster.
In-text Citation:	(Thompson, 2019, p. 43).

Article in Periodical

General Format:	Author, A. A. (Year). Title of article. *Title of Periodical, Volume*(Issue), pages. DOI
Reference List:	Ramirez, B. (2011). Having a powerful headline is important. *Modern Writers Journal, 32*(6), 4–6. https://doi.org/10.35750.30495.4506
In-text Citation:	(Ramirez, 2011)

Webpage

General Format:	Organization. (Year, Month Day). *Title of webpage.* Website name. URL
Reference List:	University of Oxford. (2021, January 20). *Organisation.* University of Oxford. https://www.ox.ac.uk/about/organisation
In-text Citation:	(University of Oxford, 2021)

OR

General Format:	*Title of webpage.* (n.d.). Website name. Retrieved Month Date, Year, from URL
Reference List:	*International Oxford.* (n.d.). University of Oxford. Retrieved February 22, 2021, from https://www.ox.ac.uk/about/international-oxford
In-text Citation:	(*International Oxford*, n.d.)

Dictionary

General Format:	Author, A. A. (Year). Title of entry. In *Title of dictionary* (Edition, p. #). Publisher.
Reference List:	Cambridge University Press. (2020). Irregardless. In *Cambridge advanced learner's dictionary* (4th ed., p. 1029). Cambridge University Press.
In-text Citation:	(Cambridge University Press, 2020)

Film

General Format:	Director, A. A. (Director). (Year). *Title of film* [Film]. Production Company.
Reference List:	Clark, K. (Director). (1990). *Awakenings* [Film]. Parkes/Lasker productions.
In-text Citation:	(Clark, 1990, 01:20:05)

TV Series

General Format:	Writer, A. A. (Writer), & Director, A. A. (Director). (Year, Month Day). Title of episode (Season #, Episode #) [TV series episode]. In A. A. Executive Producer (Executive Producer), *Series title*. Production Company.
Reference List:	Harris, H. (Writer), & Sanchez, A. (Director). (2003, October 3). Victory game (Season 2, Episode 5) [TV series episode]. In H. Allen, B. Walker, V. Nguyen (Executive Producers), *The elephant tonight*. Columbia Pictures Corporation.
In-text Citation:	(Harris et al., 2003)

YouTube

General Format:	Author, A. A. [Channel name]. (Year, Month Day). *Title of video* [Video]. YouTube. URL
Reference List:	Jones, E. [National Geographic]. (2015, December 23). *Global Warming 101	National Geographic* [Video]. YouTube. https://www.youtube.com/watch?v=oJAbAT
In-text Citation:	(Jones, 2015)

TED Talk

General Format:	Author, A. A. (Year, Month Day). *Title of talk* [Video]. TED. URL
Reference List:	Adams, C. (2019, May 23). *Possible futures from the intersection of nature, tech and society* [Video]. TED. https://www.ted.com/talks/intersection_of_nature_tech_and_society
In-text Citation:	(Adams, 2019)

Image

General Format:	Author, A. A. (Year). *Title of work* [Format]. Website name or Museum, Location. URL
Reference List:	Lewis, A. (1901). *Waking up* [Painting]. Museum of London, London, United Kingdom. https://www.museumoflondon.org.uk/museum-london/collection-work-229356040
In-text Citation:	(Lewis, 1901)

Tweet

General Format:	Author, A. A. [@username]. (Year, Month Day). *Text of tweet* [Tweet]. Twitter. URL
Reference List:	Thompson, U. [@thompdoct_1]. (2018, August 12). *You have got to be kidding...* [Tweet]. Twitter. https://twitter.com/thompdoct_1/status/346082768072582580
In-text Citation:	(Thompson, 2018)

Government Report

General Format:	Author, A. A. (Year). *Title of report: Subtitle of report* (Report No. #). Publisher. URL
Reference List:	Young, P. V. (2013). *Protecting the environment: Environmental services passion and commitment* (Report No. CH-BV 305.2). Washington State Department of Transportation. https://www.wsdot.wa.gov/reports/fullreports/305-2.pdf
In-text Citation:	(Young, 2013, p. 33)

Bible

General Format:	*Bible Version Title*. (Year). Publisher. URL
Reference List:	*The English Standard Version Bible*. (2001). Crossway. www.esv.org
In-text Citation:	(*The English Standard Version Bible*, 2001, Genesis 1:1–3

6.0 APPENDICES

An appendix (or "appendices") may be included to allow readers better understand the material in case there is a need to provide additional content that may not fit within the main text of paper.

An appendix can include following:
- Transcripts of conducted interviews (quoted in the text).
- Documents, such as questionnaires, tests, or results, etc.
- Detailed statistical data.

Therefore, there 2 main types of appendices:
1. Text appendix,
2. Table/figure appendix.

Each appendix must be referred at least once in the text.

6.1 Formatting Appendices

- An appendix should be created on a separate page after references and footnotes:
  - Label "Appendix" is:
    - At the top of the page,
    - Centered, bolded and written in title case.
  - Label "Appendix" is followed by a title on the next line:
    - Centered,
    - Describes the subject of the appendix.
- If there are several appendices, each appendix should be labelled with a capital letter:
  - For example: Appendix A, Appendix B, Appendix C, etc.

Example:

Appendix A

Subject of the Appendix

6.2 Text Appendices

- Text appendices should be formatted in traditional paragraph style.
- Beside text itself, text appendices may still include visuals, such as:
    - Tables and figures,
    - Equations, etc.
- All visuals should be named starting with the letter of the corresponding appendix and number:
    - For example, in text Appendix A with one table, the table should be labelled "Table A1".
    - For example, in text Appendix B with one table and two figures, the table should be labelled "Table B1" and figures should be labelled "Figure B1" and "Figure B2".

6.3 Table and/or Figure Appendices

Table appendix or figure appendix solely contain a table or a figure respectively:
- The title of the table or figure should be replaced with the title of the corresponding appendix:
    - For example, in table Appendix A (which only includes one table), the table should be labelled "Appendix A" instead of "Table A1".

7.0 APA SAMPLE PAPER

The APA Manual (7th edition) determines different formatting requirements for student and professional papers:
1. Papers for credit in a course,
2. Papers for scholarly publication.

These requirements mostly refer to the cover page and running head. Significantly, citation standards do not vary between the two types of paper.

For your benefit, we have given two versions of APA sample paper:
1. Student paper,
2. Professional paper.

7.1 Student Paper

Modern Period in the English Literature:

Key Points about Modern Period

Marcus White

Department of English Literature, Heldens University

ELD 1201: Modern English Literature

Dr. Korsh

April 25, 2021

Abstract

Lorem ipsum dolor sit amet, consectetur adipiscing elit. Vivamus id dapibus libero. Phasellus vel urna nisi. Orci varius natoque penatibus et magnis dis parturient montes, nascetur ridiculus mus. Curabitur ac luctus nisi, sed maximus nibh. Curabitur congue accumsan nisi, a sollicitudin turpis aliquam at. Phasellus suscipit est eget augue sagittis, ac lobortis ex egestas. Mauris vitae purus lacus. Proin imperdiet feugiat posuere. Sed a lacus aliquam, cursus sem et, faucibus nibh. Nulla diam diam, aliquam ac ante ac, blandit ultricies lectus. Sed vitae enim nisl. Praesent eu erat eget enim viverra sagittis. Nunc vel lacinia dolor, in fermentum neque. Donec consequat rutrum quam. Duis eget lacus mollis, gravida risus eu, auctor lorem. Donec sit amet libero nisi. Pellentesque sit amet ante rutrum, feugiat ipsum vel, ornare leo. Proin tincidunt purus ut massa aliquam, fermentum malesuada elit interdum. Sed posuere ut mauris non molestie. Integer nec condimentum mi, nec ornare nisi. Nulla non sagittis nibh. Suspendisse in felis at ipsum tristique pharetra sed in neque. Cras orci purus, pulvinar non placerat id, dapibus sed felis.

Keywords: Ipsum, purus, pulvinar

Modern Period in the English Literature: Key Points about Modern Period

Lorem ipsum dolor sit amet, consectetur adipiscing elit. Vivamus orci quam, iaculis faucibus risus eget, lobortis tempor ligula. Aliquam eu diam maximus, iaculis libero aliquet, volutpat nisi. Praesent nunc lorem, sodales a viverra a, placerat id leo. Praesent rutrum facilisis velit, vitae sodales eros aliquam sit amet. Lorem ipsum dolor sit amet, consectetur adipiscing elit, ligula nunc porta est, interdum pellentesque sem ligula at sapien (Harris et al., 2003). Vestibulum eu nisl erat. Cras finibus a est ac suscipit. Nullam pretium lectus nec eros dapibus, vitae laoreet ante condimentum. Donec eget efficitur ligula. Duis sed tincidunt eros, ac porttitor velit. In hac habitasse platea dictumst.

Heading (Level 1)

Nulla eu velit vestibulum, mattis nunc a, pretium metus. Vestibulum nec metus quis sem fermentum cursus. Nulla eleifend ante venenatis, placerat massa nec, dictum odio. Sed non aliquam mauris. Donec eget arcu euismod, tempor eros non, consectetur lorem.[1] Fusce ullamcorper sem ligula, sed sagittis eros gravida sed (Ramirez, 2011). Donec convallis malesuada nibh sodales suscipit. Cras molestie, arcu ac.

Heading (Level 2)

Cras at diam hendrerit, accumsan urna pharetra, rutrum ipsum. Ut pharetra, purus in finibus elementum, nulla nisi malesuada magna, quis elementum tellus arcu sit amet urna. Proin volutpat lectus non nisi aliquam venenatis. In dictum nisl eget purus posuere, eget ornare dui

---

[1] K. Peterson (personal communication, March 14, 2021) also claimed that many of her students had difficulties with APA style.

dictum. Curabitur tempus nisl sapien, ac vehicula est auctor ac. Integer iaculis nunc at risus viverra, non tincidunt nulla lobortis.

Heading (Level 3)

Praesent vestibulum sem non dictum aliquet. Donec nec dictum lacus, eu imperdiet turpis. Donec tincidunt semper sapien ut auctor. Aenean ornare ullamcorper risus a euismod. Donec maximus iaculis mi dignissim ultricies (Young, 2013, p. 33). Pellentesque imperdiet finibus neque in convallis. Vestibulum interdum euismod libero. Aliquam porttitor auctor porttitor. Pellentesque eget tortor vitae ligula accumsan semper.

Heading (Level 3)

Vivamus iaculis massa metus, at ultricies quam feugiat fermentum. Praesent placerat posuere nulla in tempor. Sed ut elit eros. Quisque. Praesent accumsan enim orci, non vehicula lorem tristique ac. Suspendisse potenti. Nunc blandit fermentum dui eget egestas. Quisque in (I. Torres, personal communication, February 12, 2020). Fusce tincidunt ornare orci, sit amet sagittis elit semper ac. Nullam interdum iaculis elit vel ultricies. Pellentesque vel magna non quam imperdiet eleifend sed tristique ligula. In eget ligula vel magna sodales fermentum nec ac nisi. Etiam dictum tincidunt libero eget rutrum. Integer ac orci quis sem sagittis vestibulum. Vestibulum ante ipsum primis in faucibus orci luctus et ultrices posuere cubilia curae.

Aliquam erat volutpat (Adams, 2019). Suspendisse erat sem, eleifend vitae ipsum vitae, auctor bibendum nunc. Suspendisse at tortor scelerisque, gravida quam ut, tincidunt massa. Quisque fermentum est justo. Vestibulum consectetur velit quis congue consectetur. Donec sed ante odio. Ut maximus enim eu felis venenatis, nec faucibus augue venenatis. Praesent finibus velit et convallis hendrerit. Ut lobortis suscipit massa, eu scelerisque tellus sollicitudin vel. Donec viverra elit nec lectus feugiat, vitae vehicula odio faucibus.

Table 1

Title of Table Title Case

Stub Heading	Column Spanner 1		Column Spanner 2	
	Column Heading 1	Column Heading 2	Column Heading 3	Column Heading 4
Table Spanner 1				
Row 1	XXX	XXX[a]	XXX	XXX
Row 2	XXX	XXX	XXX	XXX
Table Spanner 2				
Row 3	XXX	XXX	XXX***	XXX
Row 4	XXX	XXX	XXX***	XXX

Note. A general note.

[a]A specific note.

***A probability note.

Quisque purus mi, congue at facilisis et, blandit nec nulla. Integer molestie hendrerit mauris, vitae euismod metus lobortis et. Donec sapien sem, tempus ut lobortis a, ullamcorper et nibh. Thompson offered rras pulvinar eros a sapien fermentum facilisis aliquam ullamcorper ante mauris, sed condimentum eros convallis id (2018). Donec at nulla enim. Praesent turpis nisl, cursus ac arcu in, rhoncus pharetra elit. Pellentesque suscipit auctor arcu. Sed id erat purus.

Heading (Level 2)

Curabitur vel eros porta, imperdiet erat et, venenatis ante. Sed convallis nulla quis sem dapibus scelerisque. Nulla facilisi. Ut ultrices ut leo ut elementum. Vestibulum imperdiet ultricies dignissim volutpat mauris, eget tincidunt quam molestie aliquam. Aliquam diam est, porttitor ac enim sit amet, placerat pretium purus. Quisque eleifend auctor neque, sit amet fermentum elit tempus at.

Heading (Level 1)

Quisque tristique vehicula sapien posuere posuere. In maximus nisi sit amet diam dignissim commodo. Praesent condimentum turpis bibendum, molestie odio eget, convallis nisi. Duis faucibus diam non lectus iaculis, sed semper nunc elementum. Fusce iaculis, elit non porttitor faucibus, nibh arcu porttitor eros, sed suscipit nulla neque sit amet lacus. In hac habitasse platea dictumst. Cras et suscipit urna. Etiam volutpat odio (Smuggling Act, 1976). Vel lectus tristique luctus. Donec id hendrerit risus. Donec interdum turpis sit amet ligula porttitor, sit amet gravida lacus hendrerit. Aenean dignissim, tellus placerat imperdiet venenatis, ipsum odio varius eros, quis elementum quam mi id ligula. Donec tristique vehicula sapien ut molestie. Duis rutrum dapibus dui, eu aliquam erat (Martin, 2013, paras. 5-8).

Pellentesque imperdiet diam ligula, aliquam laoreet ante faucibus ut. Duis diam lectus, malesuada non sollicitudin id, pellentesque at diam. Phasellus convallis urna eget augue ullamcorper fringilla. Aenean varius eros a nibh sagittis, id mattis diam rhoncus. Vestibulum maximus tincidunt metus ac congue.

References

Adams, C. (2019, May 23). *Possible futures from the intersection of nature, tech and society* [Video]. TED. https://www.ted.com/talks/possible_futures_from_the_intersection_of_nature_tech_and_society

Bennett, B. (2014). *Methods for evaluating antimicrobial activity* (P. J. C. Hughes, Ed.). Kodansha. (Original work published 1997)

Brown, P. (1999, June 13). David Lawrence: Domestic gender violence is on the rise. *Intelligent Information Management, 9*(3), 5-7. https://intellgems.com/journal/2134499

Clark, K. (Director). (1990). *Awakenings* [Film]. Parkes/Lasker productions.

Coleman, J. (2001). *Small girl dreaming: The chocolate touch*. Bonnier Books.

Google. (2013). [Google Map of Vancouver port]. Retrieved February 24, 2021, from https://www.google.com/maps/@49.2890976,-123.1111088,17.05z

Green, A., Collins, F., Wright, D., Collins, H., Miller, B., Reed, G., Morgan, F. L., Green, V., Anderson, C., Adams, D., Li, Q., Scott, R., Hernandez, T. K., Walker, C., Baker, A. K., Evans, T. T. R., Morris, B. O., Brown, B., White, M., . . . Murphy, E. K. (2010). Molecular mechanisms underlying the evolution of the signalosome. *Science Advances, 54*(7), 22-26. http://dx.doi.org/1544.3463.4540/drky77

Jackson, V., Hill, R., & Adams, H. (2021). *Various laws on abortion around the world* [Manuscript in preparation]. Department of Medicine, University of Vancouver.

Phillips, V. C., Campbell, S., Johnson, F. T., Hall, T. Y., & Lopez, H. (2017). The Rohingya people of Myanmar: Health, human rights, and identity. *International Journal of Clean Coal and Energy, 56*(8), 23-31.

Phillips, V. C., Rogers, F. L., Green, T. D., Baker, V., & Harris, D. D. (2017). Charting organellar importomes by quantitative mass spectrometry. *International Journal of Geosciences, 1*(2), 34-56.

Richardson, B. (Executive Producer). (2018-present). *Life on Mars* [TV series]. Warner Bros. Pictures.

Rivera, H. (Host). (2019, May 18). Six heroes (No. 2) [Audio podcast episode]. In *Insider*. Short Pod Group. https://shortpod-podcast.com/

Robertson, J. K. (2020, August 25). *What does a geologist do?* [Video]. Geology. https://geology.com/articles/what-is-geology.shtml

Wright, F. R. (2015a). Branched-chain and aromatic amino acids in relation to behavioral problems among young Inuit from Nunavik, Canada: A cohort study. *International Journal of Organic Chemistry, 7*(6), 8-12.

Wright, F. R. (2015b). Chemokine profiles of interstitial pneumonia in patients with dermatomyositis: A case control study. *International Journal of Medical Physics, Clinical Engineering and Radiation Oncology, 12*(5), 6-7.

Note: This is a sample reference list. For the purpose of demonstrating a number of references, this list contains references that do not match in-text citations in the paper. Please note that in a real paper all references should match in-text citations and vice versa.

Appendix

Title of Figure Title Case

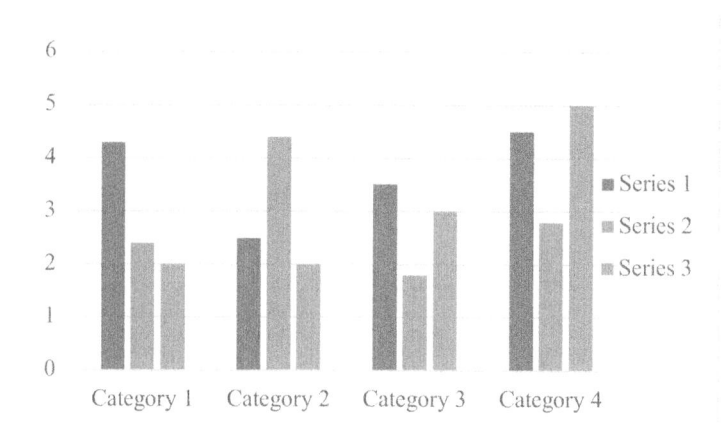

Note. General note explaining units of measurement, abbreviations, etc. or provide citation information.

7.2 Professional Paper

MODERN PERIOD IN THE ENGLISH LITERATURE

Modern Period in the English Literature:

Key Points about Modern Period

Marcus White and White Andrew

English Literature Online Lab

Department of English Literature, Heldens University

Author Note

Marcus White https://orcid.org/1257-8436-2456

White Andrew https://orcid.org/4678-8926-3324

White Andrew is now at the Department of English History, Heldens University.

We have no conflicts of interests to disclose.

Correspondence concerning this article should be addressed to White Andrew, 34 E New Heldens St., North Hollick KB 302928. Email: whiteandrew@heldens.edu

NEW PAGE:

Abstract

Lorem ipsum dolor sit amet, consectetur adipiscing elit. Vivamus id dapibus libero. Phasellus vel urna nisi. Orci varius natoque penatibus et magnis dis parturient montes, nascetur ridiculus mus. Curabitur ac luctus nisi, sed maximus nibh. Curabitur congue accumsan nisi, a sollicitudin turpis aliquam at. Phasellus suscipit est eget augue sagittis, ac lobortis ex egestas. Mauris vitae purus lacus. Proin imperdiet feugiat posuere. Sed a lacus aliquam, cursus sem et, faucibus nibh. Nulla diam diam, aliquam ac ante ac, blandit ultricies lectus. Sed vitae enim nisl. Praesent eu erat eget enim viverra sagittis. Nunc vel lacinia dolor, in fermentum neque. Donec consequat rutrum quam. Duis eget lacus mollis, gravida risus eu, auctor lorem. Donec sit amet libero nisi. Pellentesque sit amet ante rutrum, feugiat ipsum vel, ornare leo. Proin tincidunt purus ut massa aliquam, fermentum malesuada elit interdum. Sed posuere ut mauris non molestie. Integer nec condimentum mi, nec ornare nisi. Nulla non sagittis nibh. Suspendisse in felis at ipsum tristique pharetra sed in neque. Cras orci purus, pulvinar non placerat id, dapibus sed felis.

Keywords: Ipsum, purus, pulvinar

Modern Period in the English Literature: Key Points about Modern Period

Lorem ipsum dolor sit amet, consectetur adipiscing elit. Vivamus orci quam, iaculis faucibus risus eget, lobortis tempor ligula. Aliquam eu diam maximus, iaculis libero aliquet, volutpat nisi. Praesent nunc lorem, sodales a viverra a, placerat id leo. Praesent rutrum facilisis velit, vitae sodales eros aliquam sit amet. Lorem ipsum dolor sit amet, consectetur adipiscing elit, ligula nunc porta est, interdum pellentesque sem ligula at sapien (Harris et al., 2003). Vestibulum eu nisl erat. Cras finibus a est ac suscipit. Nullam pretium lectus nec eros dapibus, vitae laoreet ante condimentum. Donec eget efficitur ligula. Duis sed tincidunt eros, ac porttitor velit. In hac habitasse platea dictumst.

Heading (Level 1)

Nulla eu velit vestibulum, mattis nunc a, pretium metus. Vestibulum nec metus quis sem fermentum cursus. Nulla eleifend ante venenatis, placerat massa nec, dictum odio. Sed non aliquam mauris. Donec eget arcu euismod, tempor eros non, consectetur lorem.[1] Fusce ullamcorper sem ligula, sed sagittis eros gravida sed (Ramirez, 2011). Donec convallis malesuada nibh sodales suscipit. Cras molestie, arcu ac.

Heading (Level 2)

Cras at diam hendrerit, accumsan urna pharetra, rutrum ipsum. Ut pharetra, purus in finibus elementum, nulla nisi malesuada magna, quis elementum tellus arcu sit amet urna. Proin volutpat lectus non nisi aliquam venenatis. In dictum nisl eget purus posuere, eget ornare dui

---

[1] K. Peterson (personal communication, March 14, 2021) also claimed that many of her students had difficulties with APA style.

dictum. Curabitur tempus nisl sapien, ac vehicula est auctor ac. Integer iaculis nunc at risus viverra, non tincidunt nulla lobortis.

Heading (Level 3)

Praesent vestibulum sem non dictum aliquet. Donec nec dictum lacus, eu imperdiet turpis. Donec tincidunt semper sapien ut auctor. Aenean ornare ullamcorper risus a euismod. Donec maximus iaculis mi dignissim ultricies (Young, 2013, p. 33). Pellentesque imperdiet finibus neque in convallis. Vestibulum interdum euismod libero. Aliquam porttitor auctor porttitor. Pellentesque eget tortor vitae ligula accumsan semper.

Heading (Level 3)

Vivamus iaculis massa metus, at ultricies quam feugiat fermentum. Praesent placerat posuere nulla in tempor. Sed ut elit eros. Quisque. Praesent accumsan enim orci, non vehicula lorem tristique ac. Suspendisse potenti. Nunc blandit fermentum dui eget egestas. Quisque in (I. Torres, personal communication, February 12, 2020). Fusce tincidunt ornare orci, sit amet sagittis elit semper ac. Nullam interdum iaculis elit vel ultricies. Pellentesque vel magna non quam imperdiet eleifend sed tristique ligula. In eget ligula vel magna sodales fermentum nec ac nisi. Etiam dictum tincidunt libero eget rutrum. Integer ac orci quis sem sagittis vestibulum. Vestibulum ante ipsum primis in faucibus orci luctus et ultrices posuere cubilia curae.

Aliquam erat volutpat (Adams, 2019). Suspendisse erat sem, eleifend vitae ipsum vitae, auctor bibendum nunc. Suspendisse at tortor scelerisque, gravida quam ut, tincidunt massa. Quisque fermentum est justo. Vestibulum consectetur velit quis congue consectetur. Donec sed ante odio. Ut maximus enim eu felis venenatis, nec faucibus augue venenatis. Praesent finibus velit et convallis hendrerit. Ut lobortis suscipit massa, eu scelerisque tellus sollicitudin vel. Donec viverra elit nec lectus feugiat, vitae vehicula odio faucibus.

Table 1

Title of Table Title Case

Stub Heading	Column Spanner 1		Column Spanner 2	
	Column Heading 1	Column Heading 2	Column Heading 3	Column Heading 4
Table Spanner 1				
Row 1	XXX	XXX[a]	XXX	XXX
Row 2	XXX	XXX	XXX	XXX
Table Spanner 2				
Row 3	XXX	XXX	XXX***	XXX
Row 4	XXX	XXX	XXX***	XXX

Note. A general note.

[a]A specific note.

***A probability note.

Quisque purus mi, congue at facilisis et, blandit nec nulla. Integer molestie hendrerit mauris, vitae euismod metus lobortis et. Donec sapien sem, tempus ut lobortis a, ullamcorper et nibh. Thompson offered rras pulvinar eros a sapien fermentum facilisis aliquam ullamcorper ante mauris, sed condimentum eros convallis id (2018). Donec at nulla enim. Praesent turpis nisl, cursus ac arcu in, rhoncus pharetra elit. Pellentesque suscipit auctor arcu. Sed id erat purus.

Heading (Level 2)

Curabitur vel eros porta, imperdiet erat et, venenatis ante. Sed convallis nulla quis sem dapibus scelerisque. Nulla facilisi. Ut ultrices ut leo ut elementum. Vestibulum imperdiet ultricies dignissim volutpat mauris, eget tincidunt quam molestie aliquam. Aliquam diam est, porttitor ac enim sit amet, placerat pretium purus. Quisque eleifend auctor neque, sit amet fermentum elit tempus at.

Heading (Level 1)

Quisque tristique vehicula sapien posuere posuere. In maximus nisi sit amet diam dignissim commodo. Praesent condimentum turpis bibendum, molestie odio eget, convallis nisi. Duis faucibus diam non lectus iaculis, sed semper nunc elementum. Fusce iaculis, elit non porttitor faucibus, nibh arcu porttitor eros, sed suscipit nulla neque sit amet lacus. In hac habitasse platea dictumst. Cras et suscipit urna. Etiam volutpat odio (Smuggling Act, 1976). Vel lectus tristique luctus. Donec id hendrerit risus. Donec interdum turpis sit amet ligula porttitor, sit amet gravida lacus hendrerit. Aenean dignissim, tellus placerat imperdiet venenatis, ipsum odio varius eros, quis elementum quam mi id ligula. Donec tristique vehicula sapien ut molestie. Duis rutrum dapibus dui, eu aliquam erat (Martin, 2013, paras. 5-8).

Pellentesque imperdiet diam ligula, aliquam laoreet ante faucibus ut. Duis diam lectus, malesuada non sollicitudin id, pellentesque at diam. Phasellus convallis urna eget augue ullamcorper fringilla. Aenean varius eros a nibh sagittis, id mattis diam rhoncus. Vestibulum maximus tincidunt metus ac congue.

References

Adams, C. (2019, May 23). *Possible futures from the intersection of nature, tech and society* [Video]. TED. https://www.ted.com/talks/possible_futures_from_the_intersection_of_nature_tech_and_society

Bennett, B. (2014). *Methods for evaluating antimicrobial activity* (P. J. C. Hughes, Ed.). Kodansha. (Original work published 1997)

Brown, P. (1999, June 13). David Lawrence: Domestic gender violence is on the rise. *Intelligent Information Management, 9*(3), 5-7. https://intellgems.com/journal/2134499

Clark, K. (Director). (1990). *Awakenings* [Film]. Parkes/Lasker productions.

Coleman, J. (2001). *Small girl dreaming: The chocolate touch.* Bonnier Books.

Google. (2013). [Google Map of Vancouver port]. Retrieved February 24, 2021, from https://www.google.com/maps/@49.2890976,-123.1111088,17.05z

Green, A., Collins, F., Wright, D., Collins, H., Miller, B., Reed, G., Morgan, F. L., Green, V., Anderson, C., Adams, D., Li, Q., Scott, R., Hernandez, T. K., Walker, C., Baker, A. K., Evans, T. T. R., Morris, B. O., Brown, B., White, M., . . . Murphy, E. K. (2010). Molecular mechanisms underlying the evolution of the signalosome. *Science Advances, 54*(7), 22-26. http://dx.doi.org/1544.3463.4540/drky77

Jackson, V., Hill, R., & Adams, H. (2021). *Various laws on abortion around the world* [Manuscript in preparation]. Department of Medicine, University of Vancouver.

Phillips, V. C., Campbell, S., Johnson, F. T., Hall, T. Y., & Lopez, H. (2017). The Rohingya people of Myanmar: Health, human rights, and identity. *International Journal of Clean Coal and Energy, 56*(8), 23-31.

Phillips, V. C., Rogers, F. L., Green, T. D., Baker, V., & Harris, D. D. (2017). Charting organellar importomes by quantitative mass spectrometry. *International Journal of Geosciences, 1*(2), 34-56.

Richardson, B. (Executive Producer). (2018-present). *Life on Mars* [TV series]. Warner Bros. Pictures.

Rivera, H. (Host). (2019, May 18). Six heroes (No. 2) [Audio podcast episode]. In *Insider*. Short Pod Group. https://shortpod-podcast.com/

Robertson, J. K. (2020, August 25). *What does a geologist do?* [Video]. Geology. https://geology.com/articles/what-is-geology.shtml

Wright, F. R. (2015a). Branched-chain and aromatic amino acids in relation to behavioral problems among young Inuit from Nunavik, Canada: A cohort study. *International Journal of Organic Chemistry, 7*(6), 8-12.

Wright, F. R. (2015b). Chemokine profiles of interstitial pneumonia in patients with dermatomyositis: A case control study. *International Journal of Medical Physics, Clinical Engineering and Radiation Oncology, 12*(5), 6-7.

Note: This is a sample reference list. For the purpose of demonstrating a number of references, this list contains references that do not match in-text citations in the paper. Please note that in a real paper all references should match in-text citations and vice versa.

Appendix

Title of Figure Title Case

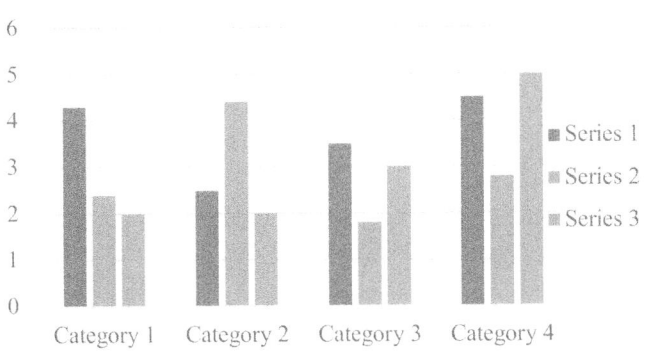

Note. General note explaining units of measurement, abbreviations, etc. or provide citation information.

SOURCES

Since the 7th edition of the APA manual is a new release, there are less supplementary resources than for the 6th edition.

American Psychological Association offers following online resources:

- APA Style Website: https://apastyle.apa.org,
- APA 7 Reference Guide (PDF): https://apastyle.apa.org/instructional-aids/reference-guide.pdf,
- APA 7 Supplemental Resources: https://apastyle.apa.org/products/supplemental-resources.

For detailed APA standards and procedures, consult the *Publication Manual of the American Psychological Association* (7th edition).

Additional Print Resources

Detailed information on APA style is available in a variety of print distributions. A large number of these resources may be accessible at Campus libraries:

- Publication Manual of the American Psychological Association (7th edition):
    - ISBN 10: 143383216X,
    - ISBN 13: 978-1433832161.
- Concise Guide to APA Style (7th edition):
    - ISBN 10: 1433832739,
    - ISBN 13: 978-1433832734.

In case you are using APA style for a class assignment, please counsel your instructor for assistance with using APA style.

Your instructor is the final authority on how to properly apply APA style guidelines in your specific case.

Made in the USA
Monee, IL
27 April 2021